The Secret Service

Theodore Rowland-Entwistle

Wayland

The Armed Forces

The Army
The Royal Air Force
The Royal Marines
The Royal Navy
The Secret Service
The Special Air Service

Cover An array of secret spying devices.

First Published in 1987 by
Wayland (Publishers) Limited
61 Western Road, Hove,
East Sussex BN3 1JD, England

British Library Cataloguing in Publication Data
Rowland-Entwhistle, Theodore
   The Secret Service. – (The Armed Forces)
   1. Intelligence service – Great Britain –
   History – Juvenile literature
   I. Title   II. Series
   327.1'2'0941   JN329.I6

ISBN 1–85210–017–6

Phototypeset by Kalligraphics Ltd, Redhill, Surrey
Printed in Italy by G. Canale & C.S.p.A., Turin
Bound in Belgium by Casterman S.A.

Picture acknowledgements
The pictures in this book were supplied by the following: Aquarius
Literary Agency 5; Camera Press 16, 17 (right); The Daily Telegraph
Colour Library *cover*, 9, 12; Radio Times Hulton Picture Library 6;
The Research House 4, 8, 14, 15, 22, 29; The Robert Hunt Library
13 (left), 26, 27, (left and right); Topham 7 (left and right), 11, 13
(right), 17 (left), 21, 24, 25. The Wayland Picture Library 10, 18, 20,
23, 28. The illustration on page 19 is by Richard Hook.

Contents

What is the Secret Service?

Every country needs to gather information about other countries that are thought to be potential enemies. This gathering of information is known as intelligence, and if it is done by secret agents it is known as espionage, or spying.

Every country must also defend itself against spies from other nations. This is called security, or counter-espionage.

Some British intelligence work is carried out by the armed forces – the Royal Navy, the Army and

An artist's impression of the P-80-1 low-altitude spy satellite. Much modern intelligence work is carried out from space.

the Royal Air Force. But there are other organizations whose main purpose is to gather intelligence. These organizations are called MI5 and MI6 and together are known as the Secret Service.

MI5, also known as the Security Service, is in charge of counter-espionage within Britain, although national security is also partly the responsibility of a section of Scotland Yard known as the Special Branch. MI5 is also involved in maintaining security within government departments.

Gathering intelligence from other countries all over the world is the work of MI6. The world of MI6 is the world of the spy, the secret agent working in another country. MI6 has been made popular in the novels of such writers as John le Carré and Ian Fleming. These exciting stories tend to make intelligence work seem much more highly coloured than it really is, although some real spies lead very strange lives indeed.

The movie image of the spy – Sean Connery as James Bond in the film Thunderball.

MI5, the Security Service

The official name of MI5 is the Security Service. Its role is to maintain the security of Britain at home by uncovering spies from other countries, and exposing British traitors. It also advises on security inside government departments, and investigates any breaches of the Official Secrets Act.

Winston Churchill (shown here fourth from left) helped to develop the security service.

MI5 began as the Home Department of the Secret Service Bureau in 1909. It was headed by an Army officer, Vernon Kell, who had a staff of one when he started. Kell was director-general of MI5 until 1940. Eight men have since held the post. Kell's organization was originally known as War Office sub-section MO5g, and was renamed MI5 in 1916.

With the threat of war looming, Winston S. Churchill, who was Home Secretary from 1910–1911, helped Kell to develop counter-espionage quickly. By the time the First World War broke out in 1914, Kell had a staff of eleven, and by the time the war ended in 1918 the number had increased to 844. During the Second World War MI5 grew even larger, but since then its numbers have been reduced.

MI5 is divided into six main branches. 'A' Branch deals with

Above *Sir Roger Hollis, a former head of M15, was accused in 1986 of being a Russian spy.*

Below *Sir Percy Sillitoe (shown right) was the director-general of M15 during the 1950s.*

administration; 'B' Branch with recruiting and checking staff; 'C' Branch with, among other things, security and sabotage; 'D' Branch with counter-espionage, especially with regard to the Soviet Union; 'E' Branch with overseas agents and international Communism; and 'F' Branch with political parties.

MI6, Secret Intelligence

Like MI5, MI6 was an offshoot of the Secret Service Bureau. It was the Foreign Section, and was at first known as Section MI1C of the War Office. Later it came under the control of the Foreign Office. It was – and still is – known officially as the Secret Intelligence Service, or SIS for short.

The first head of SIS was a naval officer, Sir Mansfield Smith-Cumming. He was known as 'C', and the heads of MI6 have been called 'C' ever since. For a long time it was usual for 'C' to sign his name in green ink, a tradition

The Secret Intelligence Service flew agents behind enemy lines during the Second World War.

which began with Cumming.

Cumming was also in charge of a new Passport Control Department, with twenty-five Passport Control Offices overseas. Many of the officials working in these offices and at the London headquarters were SIS staff. Their duty was to gather intelligence, except when they had too much genuine Passport Office work to do.

The headquarters of the Passport Control were at 21 Queen Anne's Gate in London. Connected to the rear of the building was Broadway Buildings, which housed the headquarters of MI6.

Today, SIS is organized into five sections, covering political, naval and military matters, counter-espionage and communications.

Right *An array of the equipment used by the modern spy to obtain information from a potential enemy.*

The Secret Fund

The cost of running Britain's Secret Service is met by the Secret Fund. It was set up during the reign of Charles II (1660–1685), and every year since 1797 Parliament has allotted a sum of money to this fund in the Finance Bill. How the money is spent is never revealed.

The Secret Fund is not, however, the only source of income for the Secret Service; some of its staff have other paid jobs – in one of the three armed forces for example.

The Secret Service is responsible directly to the Prime Minister, although the Home Secretary is responsible for MI5 because of its role in national security.

The Secret Fund was set up during the reign of King Charles II, shown in the centre of this picture.

The lives of Secret Service staff are complicated by the high level of secrecy which exists not only in their work but in their private lives, too. Even when they are no longer working for the service they should remain silent. The government is reluctant to allow information to be published about the Secret Service, particularly by former employees. In 1987 the government tried to ban a book by a former MI5 man, Peter Wright. Even Members of Parliament, who are usually entitled to ask questions about everything that a government does, cannot get much information about the Secret Service.

The Secret Service recruits its staff from a variety of sources, including the three Services and the Civil Service. Specialists, such as experts on foreign countries and their languages, often come from the universities.

The sum of money allotted to the Secret Fund is included in the Finance Bill which forms part of the Budget.

Codes and Ciphers

The work of spies is useless if they cannot send reports back to headquarters; and those reports would be useless if the enemy were able to read them. For this reason, agents use a variety of codes and ciphers to disguise their messages.

The armed forces and the diplomats of all countries also use codes and ciphers, and one of the tasks of the Secret Service is to try to break the codes and ciphers.

Some of the most successful deciphering work was done during the First World War. In Room 40 at the Admiralty a group of men listened to all German radio messages and tried to decipher them. They were helped by the capture of several German code books from sunken ships and submarines. These enabled them to unravel new ciphers whenever the Germans changed them. Room 40 detected all the movements of the German High Seas Fleet throughout the war.

Left *A spy places a microdot over the 'i' on this birthday card. In this way, a message can be sent home.*

After the war ended a peacetime code unit was set up in London – the Government Code and Cipher School (GC & CS for short). At the outbreak of the Second World War in 1939, GC & CS was moved to Bletchley Park in Buckinghamshire. Its greatest triumph was to break the 'Enigma' cipher used by the German forces, and it was able to read German radio signals for most of the war.

GC & CS is now GCHQ, the Government Communications Headquarters, at Cheltenham, Gloucestershire.

Below *The Government Communications Headquarters near Cheltenham, Gloucestershire.*

Military Intelligence

The intelligence collected by the British armed forces is divided into two sections – strategic and tactical. Strategic intelligence is information about the enemy which is made use of during the planning of a campaign. Tactical intelligence is confined to the immediate problem of finding out the position of the enemy's forces. It is used to decide on the course of action to take during a battle.

Up to the end of the Second World War the Navy, Army and Air Force each had its own intelligence network. Today all military intelligence comes under the Ministry of Defence.

A great deal of modern military intelligence is obtained from the air. Countries such as the United States and the Soviet Union use spy planes to fly over one another's territories to take photographs. One of the most advanced of these planes is the Lockheed SR-71 'Blackbird', which can fly at more than three times the speed of sound. Satellites in space also keep a constant vigil. They can detect

A reconstruction of a Russian dockyard made from pictures taken by an American spy satellite.

such things as the construction of nuclear missile sites.

Even aerial reconnaissance is not always accurate, however. It can be deceived. The Germans were clearly tricked at the Battle of El Alamein in Egypt in 1942. It appeared to the Germans that allied tanks and guns were concentrated in certain positions, where they could be supplied with petrol from a pipeline. They thought they spied a pipeline being laid in a trench, but what they really saw was a dummy pipe made of old petrol cans laid beside a trench.

To complete the deception the empty trench was filled in, as if a pipe had been laid in it, and the dummy pipeline was moved along to the next section where the trick was repeated. In addition, the Germans were allowed to capture a map containing false information.

The Lockhead SR-71 'Blackbird' spy plane can detect a golfball on the ground from a height of 16km.

Double Agents and Moles

It is not enough to find out all you can about another country, whether friend or foe. You also need to know how much the other country has learned about you. So secret services the world over make great use of double agents and moles.

A double agent is a person who spies for two different governments at the same time. Usually such an agent is a spy who has been 'turned' by the country he is spying against, perhaps by bribery or blackmail. Secret services use double agents to supply other governments with false or valueless information.

Moles are people who work within the Secret Service but are in the pay of another country as well. The most famous British moles include two diplomats, Guy Burgess and Donald Maclean, who

Guy Burgess, the British diplomat and Soviet spy, who fled to Russia with Donald Maclean in 1951.

fled from England to the Soviet Union in 1951 when Maclean heard he was to be investigated.

A former member of MI5, the art historian Anthony Blunt, was called in to help search Guy Burgess's flat. He took the opportunity to pocket papers which would have betrayed himself and a highly respected member of MI6, H. A. R. 'Kim' Philby. Philby came under suspicion anyway and was asked to resign. Proof of his guilt came in 1963, but Philby, then in Beirut, immediately fled to Moscow. In 1964 Blunt confessed to MI5, and was given immunity from prosecution. His confession was not made public until 1979.

Kim Philby was recruited into the Soviet spy network while at university with Burgess and Maclean.

Anthony Blunt (left) was the mysterious 'Fourth Man' in the Philby-Burgess-Maclean network.

How it all Began

The earliest reference to spies is in the Book of Numbers in the Bible. The Israelite leader Moses sent secret agents to spy out the land of Canaan, probably in about 1200 BC.

In Britain the earliest organized Secret Service was set up in the sixteenth century by Elizabeth I's Secretary of State, Sir Francis Walsingham. He provided most of the money for the spy network himself. Perhaps the best known agent of this period was the poet Christopher Marlowe, who was killed in mysterious circumstances in a pub brawl, possibly by other government agents.

Although the Secret Fund had been in existence since about 1660, it was not until the nineteenth century that most of the money was actually spent on intelligence work. Before this time the Fund was used for other government purposes, which included bribing MPs to vote with the government

Sir Francis Walsingham, who set up the first secret service in Britain, during the reign of Elizabeth I.

of the day, and providing a pension for the last Stuart pretender to the throne, Henry Stuart (Cardinal York) who died in 1807.

During the nineteenth century most intelligence work was done by amateur agents, with the exception of the intelligence work carried out in India against Russian spies. Rudyard Kipling's novel

The poet Christopher Marlowe (right) was probably a spy. He was mysteriously killed in a pub brawl.

Kim, one of the best-ever spy stories, is set in India at this time.

The modern Secret Service came into existence in 1909 when the Secret Service Bureau was founded.

The First World War

Britain had no army intelligence service for work in the field when it went to war with Germany on 4 August 1914. The very next day one was created, and a group of men was hurriedly recruited who knew French and German, and had travelled in Continental Europe. These men included schoolmasters, university lecturers, musicians, actors, artists and a sprinkling of army officers.

This unlikely group recruited Belgian refugees, men and women, and sent them back to occupied Belgium to report on German troop movements there. Women monitoring the railways took notes in their knitting – plain stitches for wagons carrying men, purl for those with horses.

Many of these Belgian agents were controlled by Victor Marie, a Frenchman who had made his living by smuggling. Reports were carried back behind the Allied

The British secret service expanded rapidly during the First World War of 1914–18.

lines by carrier pigeons. The pigeons were parachuted in crates into Belgium by plane. Victor Marie signalled to the planes when it was safe to drop the pigeons by hanging out his washing.

At home MI5 had a list of suspicious persons, which included Germans and other foreigners, as well

A First World War signals post, with its mobile pigeon loft, and carrier pigeons, on the left.

as some Britons. Using this list, any German spies living in the country were quickly rounded up. MI5 also organized censorship of mail going to neutral countries.

The Second World War

In the 1920s and 1930s British intelligence services were run down. At the start of the Second World War the Secret Service had little idea of the real strength of the Germans. The lack of good intelligence led

Much of Britain's overseas spy network was cut off by the rapid advance of the German forces during the Second World War.

them to believe that the German air force was capable of delivering a knock-out blow in the first days of the war, which it was not.

Warnings of an immediate advance of German forces into Western Europe – known as the *Blitzkrieg* – which overran the Netherlands, Belgium, Luxembourg and France, came to MI6 through the Dutch and through informers in the Vatican. This information came from Hans Oster, the chief of staff of the *Abwehr*, the German military intelligence. Oster and the head of the *Abwehr*, Admiral Wilhelm Canaris, were opposed to Adolf Hitler. Unfortunately, this intelligence was not believed.

Many of MI6's overseas stations

The British 'Twenty Committee' successfully deceived the Germans into believing that the D-Day landings would take place near Calais.

were cut off by the German advance. However, it was able to maintain a station in Switzerland, a country which remained neutral.

MI6 had considerable success in deceiving the Germans through some of their own agents who had been 'turned' by the Twenty Committee (so-called because the Roman symbol for 20, XX, was a double cross!)

This committee ran the German spy system in Britain and so could feed the Germans lots of misleading information. It successfully deceived Hitler into thinking that the invasion of Normandy in June 1944 was a diversion and that the main invasion was to take place near Calais.

Spy Swap

A spy caught in peacetime is likely to be sentenced to a very long period in prison. In wartime the penalty may be death, which is a risk spies are prepared to take.

Governments sometimes agree to exchanges of imprisoned agents. The cases of 'Gordon Lonsdale', Greville Wynne and Lieutenant-Colonel Oleg Penkovsky in the early 1960s are examples of this sort of activity.

'Lonsdale' was a Russian spy who operated in London. He held a Canadian passport, but was really a Soviet officer named Konon Molody. After months of patient watching by MI5 he was trapped and sentenced to twenty-five years in jail.

Greville Wynne was a British businessman, one of many who volunteered to find out information during business trips to foreign countries. He made many legitimate business trips to the Soviet Union where he acted as an agent for MI6.

One of Wynne's contacts was a Russian defector, Colonel Pen-

Oleg Penkovsky, the Russian spy, is shown here at his trial. He was later executed for treason.

kovsky, who gave the British valuable information about Russian espionage. But in January 1962 the Russians grew suspicious of Penkovsky. He and Wynne were both arrested, and after a four-day trial Penkovsky was executed and

'Checkpoint Charlie', a gate in the Berlin Wall where spy swaps often take place.

Wynne was jailed for eight years. Ten months later Wynne was exchanged for 'Gordon Lonsdale'.

Some Famous Agents

Robert Baden-Powell, founder of the Scout and Guide movement, was also a spy for MI6.

Many famous people have worked for MI5 and MI6, especially during wartime. One of the earliest agents was Robert Baden-Powell, later the founder of the Scout and Guide movement. Baden-Powell disguised himself as an eccentric butterfly collector and went to look at Turkish fortifications on the Dalmatian coast (now part of Yugoslavia). He drew delicate sketches of butterfly wings which were, if you looked closely, plans of the Turkish forts.

A surprising number of writers have worked for either MI5 or MI6. One MI6 recruit was Somerset Maugham, who was sent to the neutral country of Switzerland in 1915 during the First World War to pick up information from France and Germany. Maugham later wrote about his experiences in a series of short stories about a fictional agent named Ashenden.

Compton Mackenzie, who also served with MI6 during the First World War, wrote a book of memoirs in 1932 about some of his experiences. The book was banned for seven years and Mackenzie was fined £100 for betraying secret information.

Other writers who served in this

Graham Greene, who has written several spy novels, worked for MI5 during the Second World War.

section of intelligence include John le Carré, famous for his book *The Spy Who Came in from the Cold*, and Geoffrey Household, the author of the thriller *Rogue Male*.

During the Second World War a number of distinguished people were recruited to MI5. They included Malcolm Muggeridge, the writer and broadcaster, the novelist Graham Greene, and the historian Hugh Trevor-Roper.

Like Baden-Powell, Somerset Maugham also spied for Britain during the First World War.

Other Secret Services

Most countries of the world maintain their own secret services.

The United States has two organizations. The US Secret Service, set up in 1865, is a department of the US Treasury. Its job is to guard the President and other top people, and to prevent the counterfeiting of money and stamps. The Central Intelligence Agency (CIA), set up in 1947, combines the roles of Britain's MI5 and MI6. It has also engaged in subversive activities, including several attempts to assassinate Cuba's President Fidel Castro.

The Soviet Union has three intelligence units – the KGB, which is the secret police, the GRU, which is the intelligence branch of the army, and the Communist Party's own intelligence unit. The Soviet intelligence system operates in all the countries

The insignia of the Central Intelligence Agency (CIA), the American secret service.

The headquarters of the Russian secret police – the Komitet Gosudartvennoi Bezopasnosti (KGB) – in Moscow.

under Russian influence.

In France the army, navy and air force each has its own *deuxième bureau*, or intelligence unit. The roles of MI5 and MI6 are carried out by the *Service du Documentation Extérieure et de Contre-espion-nage* (SDECE).

South Africa had its Bureau of State Security (BOSS), which was set up with advice from MI5 before South Africa left the Common-wealth in 1961. It was disbanded in 1980.

Glossary

Blitzkrieg The German word for 'lightening war', used to describe the very rapid advance of the German armies in Western Europe during the Second World War.

Censorship Examining letters and any other communications to cut out any information of value to an enemy.

Cipher Method of transposing or substituting one letter for another to disguise a message.

Commonwealth Of Nations is the group of many of the countries that used to be part of the old British Empire.

Counter-espionage Detecting and combatting enemy spying.

Counterfeiting Forging or making an imitation of something, such as money, passports or identification documents.

Diplomat A government official who deals with the relations between one country and another.

Double agent A spy who works for both sides.

Intelligence Information about another country collected through spying.

Microdot A tiny copy of a secret document.

Mole A spy who is working inside the enemy's secret service.

Offical Secrets Act An Act of Parliament which is signed by everybody who works for the British government; it swears them to total secrecy about their work.

Refugee A person who has fled his or her country to escape damage.

Sabotage Deliberately damaging something belonging to an enemy.

Station In spying terms, an overseas branch of the Secret Service.

Subversive A subversive act is one which is intended to overthrow a government.

Traitor A person who betrays his or her country by spying for an enemy power.

Further Information

The Secret Service uses many abbreviations. Here are some of the most common ones:

C	Head of the Secret Service.
CIA	Central Intelligence Agency (the American secret service).
DID	Director of Naval Intelligence Division.
DMI	Director of Military Intelligence.
DNI	Director of Naval Intelligence.
GC & CS	Government Code and Cipher School.
GCHQ	Government Communications Headquarters.
KGB	*Komitet Gosudarstvennoi Bezopasnosti* (Russian secret police).
MI	Military Intelligence.
MI5	Security Service.
MI6	Secret Intelligence Service.
MI9	Escape and Intelligence Service.
SDECE	*Service du Documentation Extérieure et de Contre-Espionnage* (French secret service).
SIS	Secret Intelligence Service.

Books to Read

Non-fiction

A Matter of Trust: MI5 1945–72 by Nigel West (Weidenfeld and Nicolson, 1982)

MI5, 1909–1945 by Nigel West (Weidenfeld and Nicolson, 1981)

MI6 by Nigel West (Weidenfeld and Nicolson, 1983)

My Adventures as a Spy by Robert Baden-Powell (London, 1915)

Secret Service by Christopher Andrew (Heinemann, 1985)

Spies by Tim Healey (Macdonald, 1978)

Spies and Spying by Neil Grant (Kestrel, 1975)

Spies and Spying by David Sweetman (Wayland, 1978)

Spies – The True Story by Richard Davis (Hutchinson, 1982)

Fiction

Collected Short Stories by Somerset Maugham (Pan, 1976)

Kim by Rudyard Kipling (Macmillan, 1901)

Water on the Brain by Compton Mackenzie (London, 1933)

Index